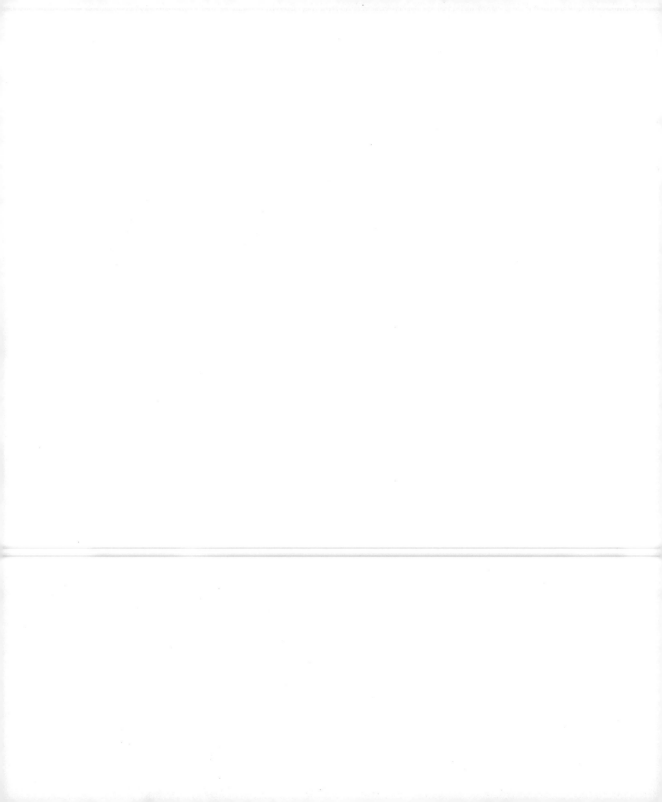

Minerals

ANN O. SQUIRE

Children's Press®
An Imprint of Scholastic Inc.
New York Toronto London Auckland Sydney
Mexico City New Delhi Hong Kong
Danbury, Connecticut

Content Consultant
Vicki Harder
Associate Professor
Department of Natural Sciences
Western New Mexico University
Silver City, New Mexico

Library of Congress Cataloging-in-Publication Data

Squire, Ann.
  Minerals/by Ann O. Squire.
    p. cm.—(A true book)
  Includes bibliographical references and index. Audience: Grades 4–6.
  ISBN 978-0-531-26144-6 (lib. bdg.) — ISBN 978-0-531-26252-8 (pbk.)
1. Minerals—Juvenile literature. I. Title.
  QE365.2.S658 2013
  549—dc23   2012008037

All rights reserved. Published in 2013 by Children's Press, an imprint of Scholastic Inc.
Printed in China 62
SCHOLASTIC, CHILDREN'S PRESS, A TRUE BOOK™, and associated logos are trademarks and/or registered trademarks of Scholastic Inc.
1 2 3 4 5 6 7 8 9 10 R 22 21 20 19 18 17 16 15 14 13

Front cover: Cave of Crystals, Mexico

Back cover: Calcite as seen under a red UV light

Find the Truth!

Everything you are about to read is true *except* for one of the sentences on this page.

Which one is **TRUE**?

T or F Most of Earth's minerals are very common.

T or F Gold is used in making computers.

Find the answers in this book.

Contents

THE **BIG** TRUTH!

Marking rock veins

4 Minerals in Our Lives

What common—and not so common—objects are made of minerals? **35**

Many of the minerals you need to stay healthy are in fruits and vegetables.

ORGANIC BABY SPINACH

ORGANIC BABY SPINACH

ORGANIC WILD ROCKET

6

CHAPTER 1

Understanding Minerals

Have your parents ever told you to eat your vegetables because they are full of vitamins and **minerals**? Maybe you have seen bottles of mineral water at the grocery store. Or perhaps you have heard about countries rich in diamonds, gold, and other mineral deposits. At first, minerals can seem confusing. How can something be in our food, in the water we drink, and in the ground?

 Iron, copper, and zinc are a few of the minerals contained in these vegetables.

What Are Minerals?

Minerals are natural substances that are found in the earth. They are **inorganic**, which means that they are not alive and do not come from plants or animals. Every mineral is made up of one or more chemical **elements**. No matter where on Earth a mineral is found, the elements in it will always be the same.

Soil is filled with the minerals plants need to live.

China mines more gold each year than any other country.

Gold is one of the most valuable minerals on Earth.

One Element or Many

An element is a substance such as oxygen or iron that cannot be broken down by ordinary chemical methods. Some minerals, such as gold, silver, and copper, are made up of a single element. Other minerals are made of two or more elements. Quartz contains the elements silicon and oxygen. Feldspar, a very common mineral, contains a number of elements, including aluminum, silicon, potassium, and oxygen.

Feldspar makes up a large portion of Earth's crust.

Many Minerals

More than 4,000 minerals have been found on
Earth, and new ones are discovered every year.
Of these thousands of different minerals, most
are very rare. In fact, only about 100 minerals are
considered to be common. The most common
minerals are those, such as feldspar and quartz,
that make up most of the rocks on Earth.

Mineral Crystals

Minerals are **crystals**. A crystal is a solid object that has flat faces, sharp edges, and angles. How a crystal looks from the outside depends on how the atoms inside it are arranged. An atom is the smallest particle of an element that can exist. Quartz is made of silicon and oxygen atoms joined together. The way these atoms are attached to each other gives quartz crystals a hexagonal, or six-sided, shape.

Quartz and other crystals often form interesting shapes.

11

Arranging Atoms

The arrangement of atoms in a mineral affects that mineral's hardness and how it breaks. For example, diamond is the hardest substance in the world. Graphite, a black substance used in lead pencils, is one of the softest. Yet both of these minerals are made of the element carbon. How is this possible?

Because graphite is so soft, it leaves marks when rubbed against paper or other surfaces.

Many of the diamonds on Earth today were formed billions of years ago.

Diamonds are one of the hardest substances on Earth.

In a diamond, every carbon atom is bonded very strongly to the atoms above, below, and beside it. These strong bonds make diamonds very difficult to break. Graphite is made up of layers of carbon atoms. Within each layer, the atoms are strongly bonded to all the other atoms in the layer. But the bonds between one layer and the next are weak. This makes it easy to split graphite along its layers, and gives the mineral a soft, slippery feel.

Erupting Volcano

Outer Crust

Magma

14

Out of the Earth

Deep below the earth's surface lies a thick layer of very hot rock. In many spots, the temperature is so high that the rocks melt, forming **magma**. Many minerals get their start in this superheated material. The process begins when magma rises up through the earth's rocky outer layer, the **crust**.

Magma can contain dissolved gasses that explode at the earth's surface, much like the bubbles in a shaken soda bottle.

Minerals From Magma

In many places, there are weak spots in the earth's crust. When the syrupy magma pushes upward, it flows into cracks and crevices between the rocks. Because temperatures are not as high in the crust as they are deeper down, the magma begins to cool. As the magma slowly cools, crystals start to form.

Fault lines are sometimes visible from high above.

Most earthquakes are caused by the sides of faults rubbing against each other.

Different kinds of granite have different coloring.

Granite

Granite is one of the most common rocks formed when magma cools. Granite contains crystals of the minerals quartz, feldspar, mica, and amphibole. It can take thousands of years for magma to cool enough to form granite. The crystals have a long time to grow, so they can become quite large. If you look at a chunk of granite, it is very easy to see the individual crystals inside it.

This rhyolite is smooth though the texture can vary.

Minerals From Lava

When magma rises all the way to the surface, it can form a volcanic eruption. This escaped magma is called **lava**. Lava cools much faster than magma that is trapped underground, so the crystals that form in it are much smaller. Rhyolite is a rock that forms from cooling lava. It contains minerals similar to those in granite, but the crystals are smaller and harder to see.

Minerals From Water

Earth's oceans, lakes, and seas all contain dissolved minerals. If the water **evaporates**, minerals are left behind. Very salty bodies of water, such as Utah's Great Salt Lake, are good places to see minerals that were formed by evaporation. One of the most common minerals formed in this way is halite, which we know as table salt.

Piles of salt form along the shore of the Great Salt Lake.

Water Underground

When magma intrudes into the crust, its heat can cause the surrounding rocks to crack. Magma contains a lot of mineral-rich water, which circulates through these cracks and deposits minerals. These deposits are called **veins**. When minerals are found in deep underground veins, mining is usually necessary to bring them to the surface.

Geologists and miners mark rocks to map out the location of veins.

Cave Minerals

Have you ever seen a cave filled with spikes hanging from the ceiling and growing up from the floor? **Stalactites** and **stalagmites** are mineral deposits formed when water containing dissolved calcite seeps through rock and drips down. When the water evaporates, calcite crystals are left behind. Stalactites and stalagmites grow very slowly—usually less than 1 inch (2.5 centimeters) each century. Given enough time, a stalactite and the stalagmite directly below it can join together in a single column.

The California Gold Rush

On January 24, 1848, James Marshall was helping build a lumber mill in Coloma, California, when he spotted a piece of shiny metal. He showed it to his employer, John Sutter, and they had the sample tested. Imagine their surprise when they found out it was gold!

Soon word got out, and people from all over the world traveled to California to make their fortunes. At first, gold was easy to find. Prospectors scooped up gravel and water into a pan and swirled it around until nuggets of gold sank to the bottom. This is known as panning for gold.

The gold rush brought thousands of people to California. In just two years, San Francisco grew from a tiny town of fewer than 1,000 people to a city of 25,000. In 1849, $10 million in gold was found in California. By 1870, when most mining had stopped, more than $2 billion in gold had been taken from California's hills!

One way to tell two minerals apart is by performing a streak test.

A

B

C

24

CHAPTER 3

Identifying Minerals

Imagine that your family bought a car and you are describing it to a friend. You might tell him some things that make your car different from others. It has two doors instead of four. It's a convertible rather than a hardtop. It's red instead of blue or silver. If you list enough of your car's characteristics, your friend could probably find it in a crowded parking lot, even though he has never seen it before.

Streak tests are usually done on special porcelain tiles.

Characteristics of Minerals

Mineralogists describe and identify minerals in much the same way. They focus on characteristics that set a particular mineral apart from others. It can take a combination of several characteristics to accurately identify a mineral. The most important mineral characteristics are streak, luster, hardness, density, cleavage, and fracture. Let's take a look at each of them.

Mining companies rely on mineralogists to identify areas rich in minerals.

Mineralogy is a specialized field of geology.

A mineral's streak can help set it apart from other minerals.

Streak and Luster

When a mineral sample is rubbed across an unglazed porcelain plate, it leaves behind a line of colored powder. This color is the mineral's streak. A mineral's visual color can be very different from the color of its streak.

Luster describes how a mineral reflects light. A mineral's luster can be metallic, like gold or silver, and easily reflect light. A nonmetallic luster might be dull, pearly, or silky.

Hardness

The harder a mineral is, the more difficult it is to scratch it. Diamond is the world's hardest mineral. Diamonds cannot be scratched or cut by anything except another diamond. Talc, a soft mineral used in dusting powder, is one of the softest minerals. All other minerals fall somewhere in between these two.

Mineral Timeline

4.6 billion years ago
Earth forms as a solid planet.

4 billion–550 million years ago
Magma trapped between rock layers begins to cool, eventually forming granite.

1812 C.E.
Friedrich Mohs develops a scale to describe the hardness of different minerals.

The Mohs Scale

In 1812, a mineralogist named Friedrich Mohs created a scale to describe the hardness of different minerals. Diamond is a 10 on Mohs' scale, and talc is a 1. Rubies and sapphires rate a 9, quartz is a 7, and gold is between 2 and 3. Every mineral has a number on Mohs' scale. Any mineral will scratch one that has a lower number and will be scratched by a mineral with a higher number.

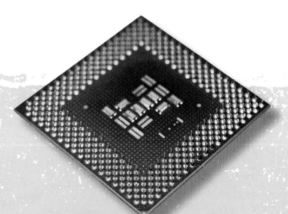

1848
Gold is discovered in California, leading to the great California gold rush.

1958
The first silicon chip is invented, paving the way for development of modern computers.

Density

Minerals are also classified according to their density. Density describes how tightly packed an object's atoms are. An object with a high density weighs more than an object with lower density. Imagine that you have two shopping bags of the same size. One is filled with feathers and the other with rocks. Which weighs more? The rocks, of course. Rocks are denser than feathers.

The same weight of copper (left) and aluminum take up different amounts of space because copper is denser.

Osmium is the densest naturally formed element.

Platinum is often used to make wedding rings.

Silver and Platinum

Sometimes, when two minerals look very similar, measuring their densities is a good way of telling them apart. Silver and platinum are both silver-colored, metallic minerals. But platinum is much denser than silver. As a result, a platinum ring will be heavier than a silver ring of the same size.

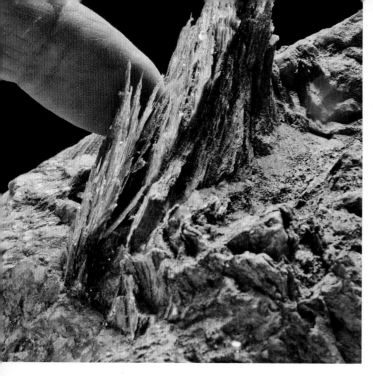

Mica often cleaves into a series of thin, flat flakes.

Cleaved minerals often create unique shapes.

Cleavage and Fracture

Cleavage and fracture describe how a mineral breaks. Some minerals, like mica and feldspar, break along a flat plane, leaving a smooth surface. This is an example of cleavage. Minerals that have cleavage always cleave, or break, in the same way. Other minerals, like copper and quartz, do not break in a regular way. Instead, they fracture, with no two pieces having the same shape.

Gold or Fool's Gold?

Pyrite is nicknamed "fool's gold" because its yellow color and metallic shine make it look similar to gold. If you know mineral characteristics, though, you can tell the difference. In streak tests, pyrite's streak is black. Gold's streak is gold. Pyrite is harder, rating 6 on Mohs' scale, while gold is 2.5. Pyrite is also much more brittle. When hit with a hammer, pyrite shatters. Gold flattens. Finally, pyrite is less dense. If a chunk of "gold" seems suspiciously light, it might just be fool's gold!

Real Gold

Fool's Gold

CHAPTER 4

Minerals in Our Lives

Have you ever heard the phrase "animal, vegetable, or mineral"? Everything on Earth belongs in one of these three categories. The first two contain objects that are or were once alive. Examples are food (meat, fruits, vegetables, and grains), clothing (wool, cotton, and leather), wood for building, and paper for writing. You can probably think of many other things that are either animal or vegetable in origin.

The wood being carved is classified as vegetable, while the tools are made of minerals. The woodworker himself belongs to the animal category.

Household Minerals

Things that come from nonliving sources belong in the mineral category. The number of objects around your house that are made of minerals is truly amazing. The toaster in your kitchen, the car in your driveway, the swing set in your backyard, and the nails and screws that hold your house together all contain minerals.

Many household appliances are made from minerals.

Even huge vehicles are made from minerals.

Transportation

Cars, trains, airplanes, and spacecraft could not
exist without minerals. The minerals magnetite and
hematite provide iron, which is used in the steel
frames of cars and trains. From chromite comes
chromium, which is used in shiny car bumpers,
trim, and door handles. The minerals bauxite,
rutile, and ilmenite contain aluminum and titanium.
These materials are used to make airplanes and
spacecraft that are very lightweight and strong.

The construction of many buildings includes the use of heavy stones.

Building Blocks

If it were not for minerals, your house, your school, and the streets and sidewalks in your town could not have been built. Gypsum is a mineral that is used in wallboard, plaster, and cement. Limestone, a rock composed of calcite and aragonite, is a popular building stone. The mineral mica is used in paints, roofing tiles, and many other items. Bricks, glass, and steel are all made of minerals.

Let There Be Light

Wolframite and scheelite are two minerals that contain the element tungsten. Tungsten is very strong and melts only at extremely high temperatures. In fact, it has the highest melting point of all metals. It's no surprise then that tungsten is used to make lightbulb filaments. This is the part of the lightbulb that is heated to give off light. Tungsten is also used to make the writing tips of ballpoint pens.

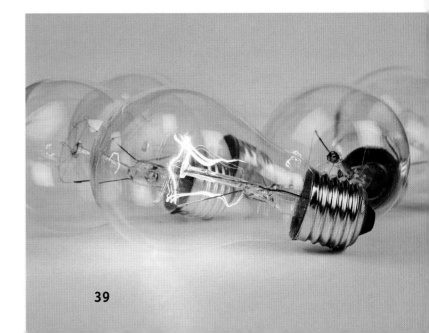

Take a look at a lightbulb close up to see minerals at work.

Minerals in Technology

Televisions, computers, and cell phones depend on minerals as well. Mica does not conduct electricity. It is used to make insulators, which protect certain parts from electrical charge. Gold, on the other hand, conducts electricity very well. It is also flexible. The

wiring and circuit boards inside your computer and cell phone may be made with gold. The glass of your computer screen and the silicon chips that control many of the computer's processes are made of the mineral quartz.

Next time you watch television, think about the minerals used to make such incredible inventions.

Fruits and vegetables are rich in minerals.

Minerals in Food

Many foods contain minerals your body needs. Dairy products and leafy greens contain calcium, which is important for strong bones and teeth. Iron—found in beans, nuts, vegetables, and eggs—helps your blood carry oxygen and is used to make protein. Magnesium, which is found in apricots, bananas, and whole grains, helps your heart beat and your muscles move. And don't forget halite (table salt). We sprinkle this mineral on food every day!

People have been using minerals to create makeup for hundreds of years.

Minerals in the Bathroom

When you brush your teeth before bed, you're using yet another mineral. Toothpaste contains the mineral fluorite, which is thought to prevent tooth decay. Bath powder contains talc, and many cosmetics contain ground mica, which gives them a sparkling appearance. And if you file your nails with an emery board, you are using the minerals corundum and magnetite.

Gems and Jewelry

Corundum is not just for nail files. It is also the mineral that we know as ruby and sapphire. Most of the world's valuable gemstones—including beryl (emerald), diamond, topaz, and purple quartz (amethyst)—are minerals. And the gold, silver, and platinum needed to turn these gems into beautiful jewelry are minerals as well. But whether they are priceless jewels or as common as toothpaste, it is hard to imagine life without minerals. Minerals are everywhere! ★

Much of the world's most beautiful jewelry is made using minerals.

True Statistics

Weight of the world's largest pure gold nugget:
156 lb. (70.76 kg), found in Australia in 1869

Percentage of all diamonds that are good enough
to be used as gemstones: 20

Percentage of iron mined each year to make
steel: 98

Amount of salt used each year in the United
States for deicing roadways in winter: 15 million
tons

Number of different minerals in the average
telephone: 40

Weight of the largest diamond ever found: 3,106
carats, or about 1.37 lb. (0.62 kg)

Did you find the truth?

F Most of Earth's minerals are very common.

T Gold is used in making computers.

Resources

Books

Hand, Carol. *Experiments With Rocks and Minerals*. New York: Children's Press, 2012.

Polk, Patti. *Collecting Rocks, Gems and Minerals*. Iola, WI: Krause Publications, 2010.

Squire, Ann O. *Rocks*. New York: Children's Press, 2013.

Tomecek, Steve. *Everything Rocks and Minerals*. Washington, DC: National Geographic Children's Books, 2010.

Important Words

crust (KRUST) — the hard outer layer of the earth

crystals (KRIS-tuhlz) — clear or nearly clear minerals or rocks with many flat surfaces

elements (EL-uh-muhnts) — substances that cannot be divided up into simpler substances

evaporates (i-VAP-uh-rates) — changes into a vapor or gas

inorganic (in-or-GAN-ik) — something that is not and has never been alive

lava (LA-vuh) — the hot, liquid rock that pours out of a volcano when it erupts

magma (MAG-muh) — melted rock found beneath the earth's surface

mineralogists (min-ur-AH-luh-jists) — people who study minerals

minerals (MIN-ur-uhlz) — solid substances found in the earth that do not come from an animal or plant

stalactites (stuh-LAK-tites) — icicle-shaped mineral deposits that hang from the roof of a cave

stalagmites (stuh-LAG-mites) — tapering columns that stick up from the floor of a cave

veins (VAYNZ) — narrow bands of minerals in rock

Index

Page numbers in **bold** indicate illustrations

About the Author

Ann O. Squire is a psychologist and an animal behaviorist. Before becoming a writer, she studied the behavior of rats, tropical fish in the Caribbean, and electric fish from Central Africa. Her favorite part of being a writer is the chance to learn as much as she can about all sorts of topics. In addition to *Gemstones*, *Fossils*, *Rocks*, and *Minerals*, Dr. Squire has written about many different animals, from lemmings to leopards and cicadas to cheetahs. She lives in Katonah, New York.